No. 178

FOURTH
PIANO CONCERTO

IN C MAJOR

Two Piano Score

By

JEAN WILLIAMS

FIRST MOVEMENT—Adagio-Alla Marcia

SECOND MOVEMENT—Scherzo

THIRD MOVEMENT—Andante Maestoso

ISBN 978-0-7935-4021-1

Associated Music Publishers, Inc.

DISTRIBUTED BY

HAL•LEONARD®
CORPORATION

7777 W. BLUEMOUND RD. P.O. BOX 13819 MILWAUKEE, WI 53213

Fourth Piano Concerto
in C Major

1st Movement
Adagio

JEAN WILLIAMS

Alla marcia (♩ = 120)

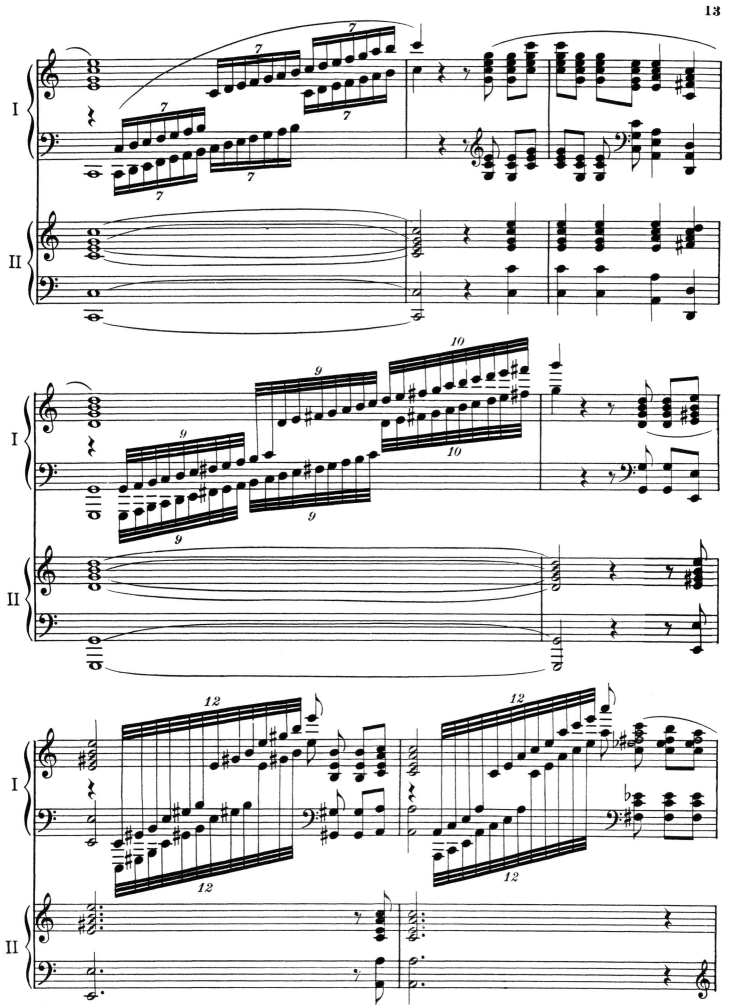

Scherzo

3rd Movement

presto brilliante